WHSmith

Practise

Spelling and Grammar

KS2 ENGLISH

Age 9–11

Brenda Stones

Advice for parents

Most parents find there's some basic bit of spelling or grammar they've forgotten: this book will help cover the ground needed to prepare for the National Tests in the upper years of Key Stage 2.

What's unusual about this book is that it links spelling to grammar.

- The book starts with key spelling rules and word-level work, moves on to vocabulary building, and then deals with grammatical parts of speech and sentence-level work.
- It also gives children techniques for collecting groups of words, so that they can enjoy discovering the patterns in spelling and grammar.
- In this way your child will gain basic confidence in using words – while also becoming aware of the many variations in the English language.
- It is probably advisable to tackle only one double page at a time, as there is plenty of content in each topic.

- The **'Get ready'** section provides a gentle warm-up for the topic covered in the unit.
- The **'Let's practise'** section is usually the main activity. This section helps to consolidate understanding of the topic. The questions in this section get progressively harder.
- The **'Have a go'** section is often a challenge or something interesting that you can go away and do which is related to the topic. It may require you to use everyday objects around the home.
- The **'How have I done?'** section at the end of the book is a short informal test that should be attempted when all the units have been completed. It is useful for spotting any gaps in knowledge, which can then be revisited at a suitable moment.
- The book ends with answers for right/wrong exercises.

First published 2007
exclusively for WHSmith by
Hodder Education, an Hachette UK company
338 Euston Road
London
NW1 3BH

Impression number 10 9 8 7 6 5 4 3
Year 2010
Text and illustrations © Hodder Education 2007

A CIP record for this book is available from the British Library.

Cover illustration: Sally Newton Illustrations
Character illustrations: Beehive Illustration
All other illustrations: Simon Dennett at SD Illustration, Arthur Pickering and Kelly Gray
Typeset by Florence Production Ltd, Stoodleigh, Devon

ISBN 978 0 340 94540 7

Printed and bound in Italy

Contents

Welcome to Kids Club!

Hi, readers. My name's Charlie and I run Kids Club with my friend Abbie. Kids Club is an after-school club which is very similar to one somewhere near you.

We'd love you to come and join our club and see what we get up to!

I'm Abbie. Let's meet the kids who will work with you on the activities in this book.

My name's Jamelia. I look forward to Kids Club every day. The sports and games are my favourites, especially on Kids Camp in the school holidays.

Hi, I'm Megan. I've made friends with all the kids at Kids Club. I like the outings and trips we go on the best.

Hello, my name's Kim. Kids Club is a great place to chill out after school. My best friend is Alfie – he's a bit naughty but he means well!

I'm Amina. I like to do my homework at Kids Club. Charlie and Abbie are always very helpful. We're like one big happy family.

Greetings, readers, my name's Alfie! Everybody knows me here. Come and join our club; we'll have a wicked time together!

Now you've met us all, tell us something about yourself.
All the kids filled in a '**Personal Profile**' when they joined. Here's one for you to complete.

Personal Profile

INSERT PHOTO OF YOURSELF HERE

Name: _____

Age: _____

School: _____

Home town: _____

Best friend: _____

My favourite:

- Book _____
- Film _____
- Food _____
- Sport _____

My hero is _____ because _____

_____

When I grow up I want to be a _____

If I ruled the world the first thing I would do is _____

_____

If I could be any celebrity for a day I would be _____

_____

1: Revising plurals

Do you remember these four easy rules for making **plurals**?

Examples

1   For most words, just add **s**: lots of **bugs** and lots of **bees**.
2   For words that end with **ss**, **sh**, **ch** or **x**, you need to add **es**, to help you say the word: one **fox**, but lots of **foxes**.
3   For words that end in **y**, you change the ending to **ies**: one **fly**, lots of **flies**.
    But if there's a vowel before the **y**, you just add **s**: one **monkey**, lots of **monkeys**.
4   For words that end in single **f** or **fe**, you usually change the ending to **ves**: one **calf**, lots of **calves**.

Get ready

1   One jelly, lots of _____

2   One dish, lots of _____

3   One loaf, lots of _____

4   One plate, lots of _____

5   One glass, lots of _____

6   One cloth, lots of _____

7   One table, lots of _____

8   One shelf, lots of _____

9   One coffee, lots of _____

10 One teacup, lots of _____

Let's practise

You may also know that words that end with **o** usually add **es** in the plural. But words with foreign roots usually just add **s**. Write the plurals of these words in the right tubs, checking your dictionary if you need to.

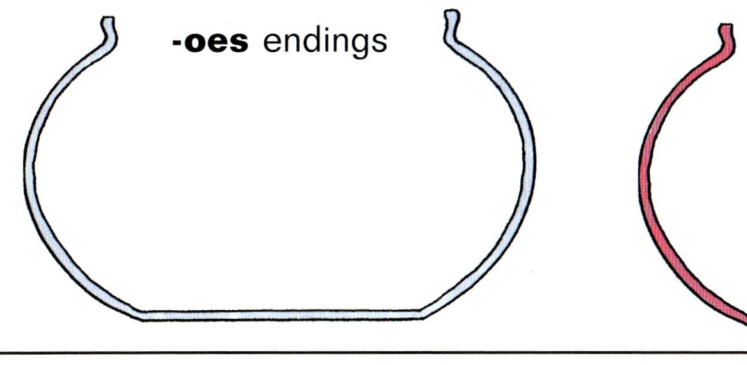

-oes endings

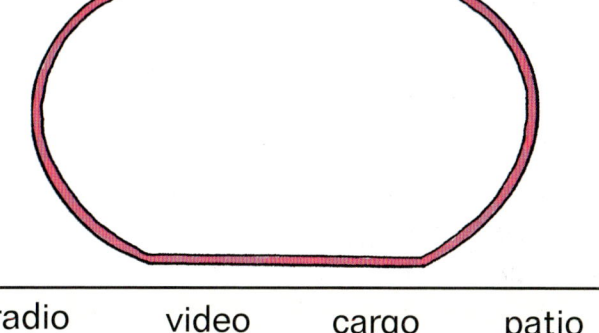

-os endings

| tomato | piano | domino | radio | video | cargo | patio |
| disco | buffalo | photo | potato | mango | stereo | studio |

Have a go

Remember the irregular plurals, like **men**, **women** and **children**?
We say one **mouse**, and a plague of **mice**.
But it's one **sheep** as well as a whole flock of **sheep**.
Then one pair of **trousers**, and one pair of **scissors**.
Make these sentences plural. (Watch out for other things you have to change, as well as the plural nouns.)

11 The man screamed as the mouse ran up his trousers.

_____

12 The woman sheared the sheep with her scissors.

_____

13 Maybe the child put the mouse up his teacher's trousers.

_____

2: Prefixes and suffixes

Do you remember how we build words by taking a **root word**, and adding a **prefix** on the beginning or a **suffix** on the end?

Examples

From **port**, meaning 'to carry', you can build **transport**, **portable** and **transportable**.

From **sign**, meaning 'a mark', you can build **resign, signing** and **resigning**.

prefix	root word	suffix
trans	port	able
re	sign	ing

Get ready

These **prefixes** all help you build new words with new meanings.

1. **Pre-** means 'before', so **preview** means _____

2. **Re-** means 'again', so **replay** means _____

3. **Im-** means 'not', so **impossible** means _____

4. **De-** means 'away', so to **derail** means _____

5. **Dis-** means 'apart', so to **dismantle** means _____

Let's practise

These **suffixes** all help to turn words into a different word class.

For each question, write a sentence using one or more of the example words given.

6 Noun suffixes: **-er**, **-ing**, **-ness**
e.g. player, playing, playfulness

_____

7 Adjective suffixes: **-ful**, **-less**, **-er**, **-est**
e.g. careful, careless, bigger, biggest

_____

8 Verb suffixes: **-en**, **-ing**, **-ed**
e.g. flatten, flattening, flattened

_____

9 Adverb suffixes: **-ly**
e.g. truly, madly, deeply

_____

Have a go

10 From the root word **hope**, what are the meanings of:
hopeful _____   hopeless _____

11 From the root word **turn**, what are the meanings of:
return _____   upturn _____

12 From the root word **migrate**, what are the meanings of:
emigrate _____   immigrate _____

3: Greek and Latin prefixes

Our language still includes bits from ancient Greek and Latin, reused in modern words. If you know what certain prefixes mean, it will help you work out the meaning and spelling of whole words.

Examples

auto means on its own, so an **automobile** runs on its own.
bi means two, so a **bi-plane** has two wings each side.
tri means three, so **triplets** are three babies born together.
micro means very small, so a **microchip** is a tiny electronic cell.
tele means distant, so a **television** shows you distant pictures.
circum means around, so **circular** means going round.
trans means across, so **transatlantic** means across the Atlantic.
aqua means water, so **aquaplaning** is skimming over water.

Get ready

Check the meanings above, then fill in the words.

1 **auto**
What's the word for an account of your own life? _____
What's the word for writing your own name? _____
What's the word for something that works on its own? _____

2 **bi**
What has two wheels? _____
What garment has two parts? _____
What's the word for cut in two? _____

3 **tri**
What has three wheels? _____
What has three angles? _____
What stands on three legs? _____

Let's practise

And here are some more:

4 **micro**
What helps you see small objects? _____
What helps you hear small sounds? _____
What cooks with small amounts of electricity?

_____

5 **tele**
What object sends you distant sounds? _____
What object helps you see distant things? _____
How do you catch someone's distant feelings? _____

6 **circum**
What's the word for a round shape? _____
What's the word for the distance round a circle? _____
What is a track that you run round? _____

7 **trans**
What carries you across town? _____
What is a human organ given to someone else? _____
What expresses words in another language? _____

8 **aqua**
Where do you keep fish? _____
What is an aeroplane that can land on water? _____
What carries water over a bridge? _____

Check the spelling on the last one, because it refers to water in the plural.

Which prefixes are Greek and which are Latin?
Check in a big dictionary to find out.

4: Spelling with suffixes

If you want to add a suffix, you need to check two things:
First, how is the root word spelt?
Second, does the suffix start with a consonant or a vowel?

Examples

1   Usually you just add the suffix as it is: play, play**ful**, play**ing**, etc.

2   For words with a short vowel sound followed by a single consonant:

*   If the suffix starts with a **consonant**, you just add it: thin + **ly** = **thinly**.

*   If the suffix starts with a **vowel or y**, you *double the last consonant* of the word: thin + **er** = **thinner**. Otherwise the single consonant would make the vowel into a long vowel sound: **pining** instead of **pinning**.

3   For words ending with **e**, like **face**:

*   If the suffix starts with a **consonant**, you just add it: face + **less** = **faceless**.

*   If the suffix starts with a **vowel**, you have to take off the root **e** of the word, so you don't have too many vowels together, so: face + **ing** = **facing**, not faceing.

Get ready

Write one word in each box, choosing a suffix to make a real word.

Root word	Consonant suffixes: -ful, -less, -ness, -ly	Vowel suffixes: -ed, -er, -est, -ing, -y
play	playful	played, player, playing
bleak		
steep		
dream		

 Let's practise

Now add suffixes to words with short vowel sounds, and to words ending in **e**. They must all be real words.

Root word	Consonant suffixes: -ful, -less, -ness, -ly	Vowel suffixes: -ed, -er, -est, -ing, -y
fit	fitful, fitness	fitted, fitter, fittest, fitting
fat		
flat		
skin		
sun		
mad		
glad		
care	careful, careless	cared, carer, caring
hope		
tune		
taste		
pale		
rude		
false		

Have a go

Riddle

It used to be (hot) _____ er,

It used to be (squat) _____ er,

It used to be (fat) _____ er,

But now it's been (flat) _____ ened.

What is the answer to this riddle?

5: The *ie* spelling

The **ie** spelling can sound like long **i**, short **i**, or **ee**. Follow the three examples below.

Examples

1   If you have a verb ending with **y** that you want in the past tense: change the **y** to an **i** and add **ed**; like **fry** and **fried**.
    (If you're adding **ing** to a verb ending with **y**, you just add it.)

2   If you have an adjective ending with **y** that you want to make comparative: change the **y** to an **i** and add **er** or **est**; like **angry** and **angrier**.
    (If you want to turn the adjective into an adverb with **ly**, you still change the **y** to an **i**, as **angrily**.)

3   And then there are words spelt with **ie** in the middle, like **field**.
    (It's usually only **ei** after **c**, as in **receive**.)

Get ready

Try the verbs first: fill all the boxes.

Root verb	Suffix -ed	Suffix -ing
cry	cried	crying
try		
fry		
spy		
rally		
carry		
marry		

Let's practise

Now try some adjectives. Add suffixes to these adjectives ending with **y**:

Root adjective	Suffixes -er, -est, -ly
angry	angrier, angriest, angrily
tasty	
icy	
shady	
merry	
bossy	
bumpy	
bushy	
bulky	
beady	

Can you fill in these words with **ie** spellings?

1 An attack on a town: s_____

2 A square of meadow: f_____

3 Your brother's daughter: n_____

4 A portion: p_____

5 For protection in battle: sh_____

6 A vicar (in church): pr_____

7 A strip along a wall: fr_____

8 The head of a tribe: ch_____

9 Short: br_____

10 To succeed: ach_____

Have a go

The rule is '**i** before **e** except after **c**'. What are the **cei** words? Fill the gaps.

Meaning	Verb	Noun
to be given	receive	receipt
to tell lies		deceit
		perception

Why are there so many ways of spelling with **c** and **k**?
We'll be **kicking cockles** in **circles** for **centuries**!

Examples

1   If you have a **hard** 'c' sound at the *beginning* of a word:
    before vowels **a**, **o** and **u**, use a **c**: as in **cat**, **cot**, **cut**
    before vowels **e** and **i**, use a **k**: as in **keg**, **keep**, **kid**, **kite**.

2   If you have a **hard** 'c' sound in the *middle* or at the *end* of a word:
    usually use **ck**: as in **rock**, **back**, **tickle**, **cackle** but sometimes **ic**,
    as in **music**.

3   When do you use a **soft c** ('s' sound)?
    Before the vowels **e** and **i** at the beginning of words, like **celery**
    and **circus**, and in the middle of words, like **musician**.

Write three words with these spellings in each tub.

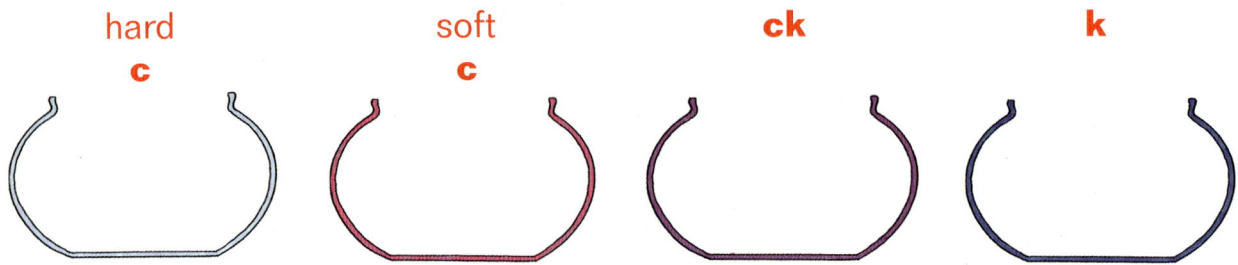

Let's practise

The ending **-ic** with a **hard c** is quite common.
Can you fill in these **-ic** words?

1. Like an angel: a_____
2. Lots of chaos: ch_____
3. Traditional: cl_____
4. Serious (measure): dr_____
5. Energetic: dy_____
6. Stretchy: e_____
7. Passionate believer: f_____

8. Very busy: h_____
9. Like an idiot: i_____
10. Mad person: l_____
11. To do with genes: g_____
12. Healthy (vegetables): o_____
13. A common material: pl_____
14. Vehicles: tr_____

Have a go

The ending **-ician** with a **soft c** is often used for people's jobs.

Can you fill in these people?

Job title	Description
b	gives beauty treatments
p	works in politics
t	looks after technical things
ph	can cure physical problems
m	a conjuror
m	plays music
op	gives you spectacles
m	works on dead bodies

I remember what **homophone** means: *same sound*, but different spelling because the words have different meanings.

Examples

Think carefully before you underline the right words here:

1.   It's (**there/their/they're**) chair because (**there/their/they're**) sitting (**there/their/they're**).
2.   The queen is (**rein/rain/reign**)ing, in bad weather it's (**rein/rain/reign**)ing, and I am (**rein/rain/reign**)ing in the horse.

Puzzling, aren't they? And if you have a spellchecker on your computer it won't help, because it can't detect a right spelling in a wrong context!

Get ready

Ring the correct spelling.

3.   That was a (great/grate) idea, and I feel (great/grate)ful.

4.   My eye-(site/sight) helps me inspect the (site/sight) of the building.

5.   My (waist/waste) may be small, but we (waist/waste) a lot of food.

6.   I (told/tolled) the vicar, but the vicar (told/tolled) the bell.

7.   (We'd/weed) better (we'd/weed) the garden.

8.   I wonder (who's/whose) asking (who's/whose) bike this is.

Let's practise

Sometimes it helps to work out which word class you need.

9 Practice (noun), practise (verb)
Let's _____ until our _____ makes perfect.

10 Advice (noun), advise (verb)
I would _____ you to listen to her _____.

11 Licence (noun), license (verb)
They've _____d us to renew this _____.

12 Effect (noun), affect (verb)
I can't tell how this _____ will _____ us.

13 It's (verb), its (possessive adjective)
I know _____ right because _____ meaning is as clear
as _____ spelling.

14 Write (verb), right (adjective)   I will _____ what is _____.

15 Passed (verb), past (preposition)
I _____ the river when I walked _____ the bridge.

16 Ate (verb), eight (number)   I _____ _____ different cakes.

17 Lead (noun), led (verb)
The stuff in your pencil is _____, but she _____ me down the path.

18 Whole (adjective), hole (noun)   That _____ is a _____ lot bigger.

Have a go

Correct the spellings of these common errors:

19 I gave him free rain. _____

20 Who's blue shoes are whose? _____

21 Waist knot, want knot. _____

8: Synonyms and antonyms

I remember these two terms:

synonyms are words that have *similar* meanings;

antonyms are words that have *opposite* meanings.

The best way to extend your vocabulary is to use a **thesaurus**.

Look up any of the words below and you'll find a good list of **synonyms**.

Many thesauruses also list opposites, or **antonyms**.

Deciding what **part of speech** you want can help you to select the right kind of word.

Get ready

List **synomyns** for these words.

1. **said**: remarked, stuttered, _____

2. **angry**: furious, mad, _____

3. **calm**: peaceful, tranquil, _____

4. **walked**: ambled, raced, _____

5. **dirty**: filthy, _____

6. **jumped**: leaped, _____

7. **horrible**: terrible, _____

8. **wet**: soaking, _____

9. **cold**: freezing, _____

10. **eat**: munch, _____

Let's practise

Now let's try **antonyms**. This time make a list of antonyms for each word, and then write a whole phrase or sentence that expresses the opposite of the original word.

11   bright
antonyms: dark, murky, black
phrase: There was <u>not a glimmer of light</u> in the basement.

12   low
antonyms: _____
phrase: _____

13   pretty
antonyms: _____
phrase: _____

14   neatly
antonyms: _____
phrase: _____

15   shuffling
antonyms: _____
phrase: _____

16   quietly
antonyms: _____
phrase: _____

Have a go

In **Get ready**, how many of the words were verbs? _____

How many were adjectives? _____

In **Let's practise**, how many of the words were adjectives? _____

And how many were adverbs? _____

9: Literary terms

We're going to teach you four special terms in literary language:
alliteration, **onomatopoeia**, **similes** and **metaphors**. .

Examples

1   **Alliteration** is when you use the same letter several times: e.g. the
    steady **st**omp of **st**odgy **st**ay-at-homes.
2   **Onomatopoeia** is when you use words that sound like the sound
    they're describing: e.g. **splishing** and **splashing** through the rain.
3   A **simile** says that something is *like* something else: e.g. Chewing
    that pasta was like munching through a telephone directory.
4   A **metaphor** says that something *is* something else: e.g. It's raining
    cats and dogs. Life is a pilgrimage.

Get ready

Try **alliteration** first. Make up phrases with these sounds:

1   **gr**:_____

2   **bl**:_____

3   **wh**:_____

4   **fl**:_____

Let's practise

Similes and metaphors sound like very nasty diseases to me!

Try inventing some **similes** and **metaphors**.

5   Invent a simile for **hair**:
like _____

6   Invent a simile for **soup**:
like _____

7   Invent a simile for **dancing**:
like _____

8   Invent a metaphor for **traffic**:
_____

9   Invent a metaphor for **skyscrapers**:
_____

10 Invent a metaphor for **crowds**:
_____

Have a go

And lastly **onomatopoeia**; write words that sound:

11 **loud**:_____

12 **slimy**:_____

13 **wet**:_____

14 **swooping**:_____

10: Greek and Latin roots

You remember we did Greek and Latin prefixes in Unit 3?

Now we're going to look at more English words with Greek and Latin origins, to help you spell them and understand their meaning.

Examples

If you have a good dictionary, it should tell you the **origin** or **derivation** of words that were originally Greek or Latin. Here's an example:

school

Word origin: from a Greek word *skhole*, which originally meant 'leisure' and later 'place for having discussions'. In ancient Greece, discussing things was an important way of using leisure time.

Get ready

First, here are some Latin words.

1 **audi** means to hear.
What does audio-visual mean? _____
And audible? _____
And audience? _____

2 **credo** means I believe.
What does credible mean? _____
And incredible? _____

3 **primus** means first.
What does primary school mean? _____
And primrose? _____
And Prime Minister? _____

4 **pedes** means foot.
What does pedestrian mean? _____
And pedicure? _____
And pedal? _____

Let's practise

Now try these Greek words.

5 **logos** means study.
What is the study of the influence of stars? *astr*_____
What is the study of living things? *bio*_____
What is the study of meteors and weather? *met*_____

6 **graph** means written.
What's the word for writing your own name? *auto*_____
What's the word for distant writing? *tele*_____
And what do you think graphology is? _____

7 **photo** means light.
What does photograph mean? _____
What is a telephoto lens? _____
What does photosensitive mean? _____

8 **scope** means look at.
What does a microscope do? _____
What does a telescope do? _____
What does a periscope do? _____

9 **phobia** means fear.
Water is **hydro**, so what does hydrophobia mean? _____
And claustrophobia? _____
And agoraphobia? _____

Have a go

Sometimes the plurals are spelt according to the rules of the original language. Can you fill in these?

Word	Origin	Meaning	Plural
cactus	Latin	desert plant	
fungus	Latin	mushrooms, toadstools, etc.	
radius	Latin	line from the centre of a circle	
polyhedron	Greek	shape with many sides	

11: Old and new words

The English language has taken in words from all over the world, and it's changing all the time.

Examples

1   We've looked at ancient roots, from Greek and Latin, like **graph** and **credo**.
2   Then there are old English usages, as you might find in Shakespeare's language, like **hither** and **yon**.
3   Then there have been gradual additions from other languages, like **bazaar** and **boutique**.
4   And finally there are brand new words, like **cyber** and **blog**.

Also, a lot of words get recycled with different meanings, like **data** or **spin**, which have ancient roots but new uses.

Get ready

Do you know what these very new words mean? You can look them up online or in a dictionary.

New word	Meaning
flak	anti-aircraft fire. The word comes from the initials of Flieger Abwehr-Kanone.
cyberspace	
banoffi	
blog	
bungee	
download	
edutainment	
geek	
karaoke	
spam	
spin	
surf	

Let's practise

Here we've told you which languages these words come from.

Can you fill in their meanings?

Word	Origin	What is it?
spaghetti	Italian	long strings of pasta
paparazzi	Italian	
confetti	Italian	
graffiti	Italian	
bungalow	Hindi	
juggernaut	Hindi	
khaki	Persian	
bazaar	Persian	
boutique	French	
brouhaha	French	
chic	French	
niche	French	
anorak	Eskimo	
chaos	Greek	
delicatessen	German	

Have a go

And finally here are some old words that you might find in plays written by Shakespeare, for instance. Can you fill in their meanings?

Old word	Meaning
yonder	
thither	
whither	
thou hast	
thou wast	

12: Direct and reported speech

There are two ways of writing down the words people say:
either in **direct speech**, which means using **speech marks**;
or else in **reported speech**, which means reporting the words afterwards.

Examples

1 **Direct speech** has trickier punctuation, so here's a model:
"When does the bus go?" she asked.
"At half past eight," he answered.
"Oh dear," she wailed, "that means I've missed it then."
He cheered her up by saying, "But there'll be another one along soon."

2 And here's the same conversation in **reported speech**:
She asked when the bus went.
He told her it went at half past eight.
She was upset that she'd therefore probably missed it.
But he reassured her that there would be another one along soon.

Here are some rules for **direct speech** (DS) and **reported speech** (RS).
Draw lines to join each rule to an example above.

DS1 Start a new line for each speech.
DS2 The speech always begins with a capital letter, even after an introductory phrase.
DS3 But if the speech is interrupted, it carries on with a small letter.
DS4 The end punctuation goes inside the speech marks.

RS1 You don't have to start a new line for each speech (though we have here just to make the comparison easier).
RS2 The tenses all go back in time, because they are being reported afterwards.
RS3 You might well change the verbs used, as they are not describing actual speech any more.
RS4 What was first person within the direct speech becomes third person in the reported speech.

Let's practise

Here is part of a playscript.
Rewrite it first as direct speech, then as reported speech.

JAMELIA:	Hey, I want to show you something!
AMINA:	What is it?
JAMELIA:	I'm not telling you. It's a secret.
AMINA:	Where is it then?
JAMELIA:	Back home. Come round and I'll show you.

1 Direct speech: _____

_____

_____

_____

_____

_____

2 Reported speech: _____

_____

_____

_____

_____

_____

Have a go

Write your own report of a conversation, e.g. a discussion about school dinners.

13: Changing parts of speech

Another use of suffixes is to change verbs into nouns, or nouns and adjectives into verbs.

Examples

It all goes back to building on root words again:

1   Common **noun** endings are **-ation**, **-tion**, **-sion**, as in **formation**, **direction**, **tension**.
2   Common **verb** endings are **-ise**, **-ify**, **-en**, as in **liquidise**, **clarify**, **harden**.

 **Get ready**

Use the right endings to make each of these verbs into a noun.
Then write the nouns in the correct tubs.
There should be exactly the same number of words in each tub.

add	divide	organise	subtract	digest
dictate	explode	educate	direct	
multiply	confuse	form	expand	deduce	exclude

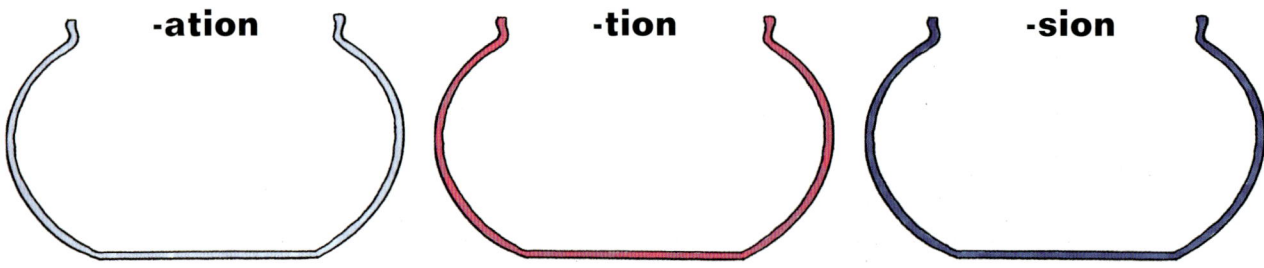

-ation   -tion   -sion

Let's practise

Fill in the word class of the root word, and then make new verbs. But beware, you often have to change the spellings!

Root word	Word class	Ending	Verb
liquid	noun	-ise	liquidise
vapour		-ise	
harmony		-ise	
glory	noun	-ify	glorify
solid		-ify	
clear		-ify	
horror		-ify	
terror		-ify	
just		-ify	
awake	adjective	-en	awaken
damp		-en	
deaf		-en	
deep		-en	
fat		-en	
less		-en	
loose		-en	
red		-en	

Have a go

What rules would you write for turning adjectives into verbs with **-en**?

If the adjective has a short vowel sound followed by a single consonant,

_____.

If the adjective ends in **e**, _____.

We're going to show you two more kinds of verbs: **imperatives** for giving orders, and **passives** for formal language.

Examples

1 You use **imperatives** to give an order or an instruction.
   Shut the door! **Turn** left! **Put** it outside!
   You therefore find imperatives in any kind of instructive writing,
   e.g. recipes, rules for games, directions.
2 You use **passive** verbs to describe actions 'being done': Active:
   I kick the ball into touch.
   Passive: The ball **is kicked** into touch.
   You use the passive for explanations, or in formal writing.

Get ready

1   Highlight the **imperatives**.

Draw some monkeys on cardboard.

Give them curled tails to swing from.

If you make a mistake, rub it out and try again.

Colour the monkeys in bright colours.

Cut them out.

Go carefully round the corners!

Hang them on the end of your bed, or a baby's cot.

2   What do you notice about the imperatives?

Are they different for singular and plural? _____

Do they have present tense and past tense? _____

Do they have special endings? _____

The answers here are all No. Imperatives are simple to write because they never change.

Let's practise

3 Highlight the **passive** verbs in this explanation.

Bread is made from wheat, or sometimes from rye.
The cereal is sown by farmers in the spring and harvested in the autumn.
The seeds are then separated from the ears of corn.
The seeds are ground to make flour.
The flour is transported to the bakery.
The bakers then use the flour to bake bread.
The bread is sold to us through bakeries or supermarkets.

4 Rewrite the explanation above using **active** verbs.

_____

_____

_____

_____

_____

_____

_____

Have a go

5 What do you notice about the **passive** verbs?

How many words do you need for a passive verb? _____

What is the first part of the verb? _____

Where is the subject of the verb? _____

6 What do you notice about the **active** verbs?

What goes before the verb? _____

How many words are the verbs made up of? _____

What tense are they? _____

15: Pronouns

Let's do a reminder about the right form of **pronouns**.

> **Examples**
>
> 1   *Subjects and objects*
> When do you say 'The king and **I**' and when is it 'The king and **me**'?
> Work it out by taking the other person away, and seeing if you'd then say
> **I** or **me**.
> * The queen invited the king and **me** for breakfast. (She invited
>   **me** . . .)
> * The king and **I** accepted the invitation. (**I** accepted . . .)
> You usually use **I** before a verb, and **me** after a verb.
> **I** is called the **subject** of the verb; **me** is called the **object** of the verb.
>
> 2   *Possessives*
> * This is **my** diary; it's completely **mine**.
> * If that's **your** diary, then it's **yours**.
> * Of course **our** diary is **ours**.
> Here you'll see that the possessive is different when it stands on its own.
> * The examples in the first part of each sentence are called **possessive**
>   **adjectives**, as they describe a noun (**diary**).
> * The examples in the second part of each sentence are called
>   **possessive pronouns**, as they stand alone.
> And you never use an apostrophe with any of these possessives.

Get ready

Can you fill in the right pronouns for subjects and objects?

	Singular subject	Singular object	Plural subject	Plural object
1st person	I	me		us
2nd person	you		you	
3rd person	he, she, it	him, her, it	they	

Let's practise

Subject and object pronouns

Fill the gaps.

1. My friend and (I/me) _____ are going out to the park.

2. Our other friends saw her and (I/me) _____ on the way.

3. They said they'd meet her and (me/I) _____ on the way back.

4. They invited (we/us) _____ back to their place.

5. We thanked him and (she/her) _____ for the invitation.

Possessives

Fill the gaps.

6. She said the book was (belonging to her) _____.

7. I said the book was (belonging to me) _____.

8. She said she knew from (belonging to it) _____ cover that it was (belonging to her) _____.

9. We agreed to ask our friends if it was (belonging to them) _____.

10. They said that (belonging to them) _____ feeling was that it was not (belonging to them) _____.

Have a go

	Singular possessive adjective	Singular possessive pronoun	Plural possessive adjective	Plural possessive pronoun
1st person	my		our	
2nd person	your			yours
3rd person	his, her, its	his, hers	their	

16: Prepositions

I remember that **prepositions** are to do with positions.

Examples

1   Prepositions are all those little words that describe where something is: **above**, **below**, **behind**, **near**, **on**, **under**, **past**, **through**, etc.

2   You can sometimes add prepositions to verbs, to change their meaning: **look**, **look up**, **look up to**, **look down on**.

3   Some prepositions are more abstract, describing *relative* position: e.g. different **from**, similar **to**, better **than**, compare **with**, prefer **to**.

4   And then there are longer **prepositional phrases**: e.g. **next to**, **not far from**, **in the neighbourhood of**, **round about**.

Get ready

Try playing I-spy with a mystery object in your room.
Think of an object, and write five sentences to say where it is.
Use a different preposition for each sentence.

1 _____

2 _____

3 _____

4 _____

5 _____

Now show this page to someone at home.
Can they guess where and what the object is?

Let's practise

Give meanings for all these verbs with prepositions:

1. look up _____

2. look up to _____

3. look down on _____

4. give up _____

5. give in _____

6. give back _____

7. speak up _____

8. speak out _____

9. feed back _____

10. stand down _____

11. get up _____

12. get on _____

13. get back _____

14. run out of _____

15. run up _____

16. run off _____

Have a go

Fill in the gaps.

17. This year is different _____ last year.

18. It's more similar _____ the year before.

19. I'd compare it _____ next year.

20. I prefer this year _____ last year.

21. Overall this year is better _____ all the years before.

17: Connectives

I can guess what **connectives** do:
they connect up sentences.

Examples

1 **Connectives of time** are often used at the beginning of sentences to stress the sequence of time: e.g. **first**, **then**, **after**, **before**, **next**. They are used especially in chronological reports.

2 **Connectives of cause** can be used either at the beginning of sentences or to join two sentences: e.g. **and**, **but**, **however**, **whereas**, **because**, **if**, **although**. They are also used in reports and in explanations.

Get ready

Here are five ways of linking these two sentences:

The cat ate five pizzas. The cat was sick.

❶   The cat ate five pizzas **and then** was sick.

❷   The cat ate five pizzas **and so** it was sick.

❸   The cat was sick **as a result of** eating five pizzas.

❹   **Because** the cat ate five pizzas, it was sick.

❺   **After** the cat ate five pizzas, it was sick.

What do you notice?

❶   Where can the connectives go? _____

❷   Which connectives are about time? _____

❸   Which connectives are about cause? _____

❹   Which sentences use pronouns? _____

Let's practise

Newspaper report

A journalist has gathered these six statements from witnesses.
Sort them into the best sequence for a news report by numbering the statements.

A shopkeeper saw a car mounting the pavement.

No one caught the number of the car.

A cyclist saw a pushchair being knocked into the road.

A young lad called the ambulance on his mobile.

A pedestrian saw a car approaching very fast.

Another driver said he saw a car driving away very fast.

Then write up your report, adding connectives to stress the sequence.

1 _____

2 _____

3 _____

4 _____

5 _____

6 _____

Write two ways of connecting these two sentences:

I am listening to music. I am doing my homework.

18: Clauses and phrases

This last topic is about building sentences from **clauses** and **phrases**.

Examples

1   Here is a sentence made up of two clauses, joined with a connective:
I am listening to music, while I am doing my homework.
Every **clause** has to have a verb.

2   If there's more than one clause, as above, one has to be the **main clause**. The main clause is the one that can stand *on its own*.
So the main clause above is **I am listening to music**, because 'while I am doing my homework' doesn't make sense on its own.

3   The clauses that aren't main clauses are called **subsidiary clauses**. They usually start with a connective, like **while** above.

4   We could add another part to the sentence, this time without a verb:
I am listening to music, **on the radio**, while I am doing my homework.
We call **on the radio** a **phrase**, not a clause, because it has *no verb*.

Underline all the **main clauses** in red.

1   The cat ate five pizzas and then was sick.

2   The cat ate five pizzas and so it was sick.

3   The cat was sick as a result of eating five pizzas.

4   Because the cat ate five pizzas, it was sick.

5   After the cat ate five pizzas, it was sick.

 **Let's practise**

Underline the **verbs in the clauses** in red.
Underline the **phrases** in blue.

6 My grandmother gave me the money, because it was my birthday.

7 I wrote my grandmother a thank-you letter, or rather I sent her a text.

8 I'm saving up for new boots, which I'll buy at the same superstore.

9 It'll be next year before I have enough money.

10 Do you know how much those boots cost in the sale?

11 I don't expect that I can afford them, especially the black ones.

 **Have a go**

Now write out all the **subsidiary clauses** from above.
You should be selecting from all the clauses with verbs underlined in red.

12 _____

13 _____

14 _____

15 _____

16 _____

17 _____

Lastly, underline the connectives at the beginning of these subsidiary clauses in green.

How have I done?

SPELLING

1 Write the plurals of:
batch _____, folly _____, donkey _____,
stereo _____, dress _____, half _____.

2 Add prefixes to make new words:
_____vent, _____tend, _____take,
_____possible, _____soluble, _____helpful.

3 Add the suffix **-ing**:
(help/ing) _____, (play/ing) _____, (bat/ing) _____,
(hope/ing) _____, (hop/ing) _____, (shop/ing) _____.

4 Add the suffix **-ed**:
(play/ed) _____, (hop/ed) _____, (hope/ed) _____,
(bat/ed) _____, (wilt/ed) _____, (fail/ed) _____.

5 Add suffixes to these words ending in **y**:
She (carry/ed) _____ her things (angry/ly) _____ down the
steep path, (hurry/ing) _____ (busy/ly) _____.

6 Add **ie** or **ei** in the middle of these words:
rec_____ve, dec_____ve, s_____ze, s_____ge, sh_____ld, p_____ce.

7 Make nouns ending in **-tion** or **-sion** from these verbs:
abolish _____, extend _____, intend _____,
add _____, multiply _____, divide _____.

8 Fill in the jobs of people who work in these areas:
music _____, magic _____, beauty _____.

9 Choose the right spelling of **it's/its**:
_____ clear that _____ not enough to know if _____
meaning is clear; _____ also important to know how _____ spelt.

10 Choose the right spelling of **who's/whose**:
I will ask _____ playing tonight, so that I can check _____
boots are needed, and _____ shirts.

GRAMMAR

11 Write this dialogue in reported speech:
"Where is all this leading us?" he asked.
"It's helping us to write better," she answered.

_____

_____

12 Write this passage using passive verbs.
The cows eat grass. The farmers milk the cows. The farmers send the milk to the dairy. The dairy puts the milk in cartons. We buy the milk from shops.

_____

_____

13 Now rewrite the original passage from question **12** as two sentences, using connectives.

_____

_____

_____

14 Now rewrite the original passage from question **12**, replacing the noun 'milk' with a pronoun.

_____

_____

_____

15 What word class can each of these words be? It's often more than one.

Solid _____

Through _____

Past _____

Bat _____

Answers

UNIT 1
Get ready
1 jellies 2 dishes 3 loaves 4 plates 5 glasses
6 cloths 7 tables 8 shelves 9 coffees
10 teacups

Let's practise
- o e s: tomatoes, potatoes, buffaloes, cargoes, mangoes, dominoes
- o s: patios, discos, pianos, photos, radios, videos, stereos, studios

Have a go
11 The men screamed as the mice ran up their trousers.
12 The women sheared the sheep with their scissors.
13 Maybe the children put the mice up their teachers' trousers.

UNIT 2
Get ready
1 looking at before 2 play again 3 not possible
4 come away from the rails 5 take apart
6–9 any imaginative answer

Have a go
10 full of hope, without hope
11 come back, turn upwards
12 move away, move into

UNIT 3
Get ready
1 autobiography, autograph, automatic
2 bicycle, bikini, bisect
3 tricycle, triangle, tripod

Let's practise
4 microscope, microphone, microwave
5 telephone, telescope, telepathy
6 circle, circumference, circuit
7 transport, transplant, translation
8 aquarium, aquaplane, aqueduct

Have a go
Greek: auto, tri, micro, tele
Latin: bi, circum, trans, aqua

UNIT 4
Get ready
Any of the following:

Root word	Consonant suffixes	Vowel suffixes
bleak	bleakness, bleakly	bleaker, bleakest
steep	steepness, steeply	steeped, steeper, steepest
dream	dreamless	dreamed, dreamer, dreaming, dreamy

Let's practise

Root word	Consonant suffixes	Vowel suffixes
fat	fatless, fatness	fatter, fattest, fatty
flat	flatness, flatly	flatter, flattest
skin	skinful, skinless	skinned, skinning, skinny
sun	sunless	sunned, sunning, sunny
mad	madness, madly	madder, maddest
glad	gladness, gladly	gladder, gladdest
care	careful, careless	cared, carer, caring
hope	hopeful, hopeless	hoped, hoping
tune	tuneful, tuneless	tuned, tuner, tuning
taste	tasteful, tasteless	tasted, taster, tasting, tasty
pale	paleness, palely	paled, paler, palest, paling
rude	rudeness, rudely	ruder, rudest
false	falseness, falsely	falser, falsest

Have a go
hotter, squatter, fatter, flattened
A squashed chilli pepper!

UNIT 5
Get ready

Root verb	Suffix -**ed**	Suffix -**ing**
try	tried	trying
fry	fried	frying
spy	spied	spying
rally	rallied	rallying
carry	carried	carrying
marry	married	marrying

Let's practise

Root adjective	Suffix -**er**	-**est**	-**ly**
tasty	tastier	tastiest	tastily
icy	icier	iciest	icily
shady	shadier	shadiest	shadily
merry	merrier	merriest	merrily
bossy	bossier	bossiest	bossily
bumpy	bumpier	bumpiest	bumpily
bushy	bushier	bushiest	bushily
bulky	bulkier	bulkiest	bulkily
beady	beadier	beadiest	beadily

1 siege 2 field 3 niece 4 piece 5 shield 6 priest
7 frieze 8 chief 9 brief 10 achieve

Have a go

Meaning	Verb	Noun
to tell lies	deceive	deceit
to see	perceive	perception

UNIT 6
Let's practise

1 angelic 2 chaotic 3 classic 4 drastic 5 dynamic
6 elastic 7 fanatic 8 hectic 9 idiotic 10 lunatic
11 genetic 12 organic 13 plastic 14 traffic

Have a go

beautician, politician, technician, physician, magician, musician, optician, mortician

UNIT 7
Examples

1 their, they're, there
2 reigning, raining, reining

Get ready

3 great, grateful
4 eyesight, site
5 waist, waste
6 told, tolled
7 We'd, weed
8 who's, whose

Let's practise

9 practise, practice
10 advise, advice
11 licensed, licence
12 effect, affect
13 it's, its, its
14 write, right
15 passed, past
16 ate, eight
17 lead, led
18 hole, whole

Have a go

19 I gave him free rein.
20 Whose blue shoes are whose?
21 Waste not, want not.

UNIT 8
Have a go

4 verbs, 6 adjectives
4 adjectives, 2 adverbs

UNIT 10
Get ready

1 for hearing and seeing, can be heard, people who hear
2 believable, unbelievable
3 first school, first rose of spring, first minister
4 person on foot, looking after your feet, what you push with your foot

Let's practise

5 astrology, biology, meteorology
6 autograph, telegraph, study of handwriting
7 print from light, distant light, sensitive to light
8 look at small things, look at distant things, look at things around you
9 fear of water, fear of being closed in, fear of open spaces

Have a go

cacti, fungi, radii, polyhedra

UNIT 11
Get ready
cyberspace – the Internet

banoffi – banana and toffee

blog – web log, or online journal

bungee – jumping from a height, attached to an elastic rope

download – to take off the internet

edutainment – mixture of education and entertainment

geek – unsociable person interested in particular hobbies

karaoke – miming to music

spam – junk e-mails

spin – giving something a good image

surf – to browse the internet

Let's practise
paparazzi – photographers who chase celebrities

confetti – what you throw at weddings

graffiti – writing on buildings/walls

bungalow – single-storey house

juggernaut – historically, a large chariot in a procession; now a lorry

khaki – dust-coloured

bazaar – market

boutique – small shop selling fashionable clothes

brouhaha – lot of noise

chic – smart

niche – small corner, or special position

anorak – winter jacket with hood

chaos – confusion

delicatessen – shop selling nice things to eat

Have a go
yonder –	over there
thither –	to there
whither –	to where
thou hast –	you have
thou wast –	you were

UNIT 12
Let's practise
1 Jamelia called out to Amina, "Hey, I want to show you something!"

"What is it?" asked Amina.

"I'm not telling you," replied Jamelia. "It's a secret."

"Where is it then?" asked Amina.

"Back home," said Jamelia. "Come round and I'll show you."

2 Jamelia called to Amina that she wanted to show her something. Amina asked what it was, but Jamelia would not tell her, because it was a secret. Amina then asked where it was. Jamelia replied that it was at her house. She invited Amina round so that she could show it to her.

UNIT 13
Get ready
-*ation*: organisation, formation, dictation, education, multiplication

-*tion*: addition, deduction, digestion, direction, subtraction

-*sion*: confusion, division, exclusion, expansion, explosion

Let's practise
Root word	Word class	Ending	Verb
vapour	noun	-ise	vaporise
harmony	noun	-ise	harmonise
solid	noun/adjective	-ify	solidify
clear	adjective	-ify	clarify
horror	noun	-ify	horrify
terror	noun	-ify	terrify
just	adjective	-ify	justify
damp	adjective	-en	dampen
deaf	adjective	-en	deafen
deep	adjective	-en	deepen
fat	adjective	-en	fatten
less	adjective	-en	lessen
loose	adjective	-en	loosen
red	adjective	-en	redden

Have a go
1 If the adjective has a short vowel sound followed by a single consonant, double the last consonant and add -*en*.

2 If the adjective ends in *e*, remove the *e* and add -*en*; or just add *n*.

UNIT 14
Get ready
1 Draw, Give, rub, try, Colour, Cut, Go, Hang

Let's practise
3 is made, is sown, [is] harvested, are separated, are ground, is transported, is sold

4 We make bread from wheat, or sometimes from rye.
Farmers sow the cereal in the spring and harvest it in the autumn.
They separate the seeds from the ears of corn.
People grind them to make flour.
Drivers transport the flour to the bakery.
The bakers then use the flour to bake bread.
Bakeries and supermarkets sell us the bread.

Have a go
5 two words is/are at the beginning of the sentence
6 Active a subject one word present tense

UNIT 15
Get ready

	Singular subject	Singular object	Plural subject	Plural object
1st person	I	me	we	us
2nd person	you	you	you	you
3rd person	he, she, it	him, her, it	they	them

Let's practise
1 I 2 me 3 me 4 us 5 her
6 hers 7 mine 8 its hers 9 theirs 10 their theirs

Have a go

	Singular possessive adjective	Singular possessive pronoun	Plural possessive adjective	Plural possessive pronoun
1st person	my	mine	our	ours
2nd person	your	yours	your	yours
3rd person	his, her, its	his, hers	their	theirs

UNIT 16
Let's practise
1 research
2 respect
3 despise
4 don't know, stop trying
5 surrender
6 return
7 speak louder
8 give an opinion
9 give comments
10 give up your position
11 stand up, get out of bed
12 make progress
13 return
14 have none left
15 calculate a bill, or debts
16 escape

Have a go
17 from 18 to 19 with 20 to 21 than

UNIT 17
Get ready
1 beginning or middle of the sentence
2 and then, after
3 and so, as a result of, because
4 2, 4, 5

Let's practise
Before adding the connectives:
1 A pedestrian saw a car approaching very fast.
2 A shopkeeper saw a car mounting the pavement.
3 A cyclist saw a pushchair being knocked into the road.
4 A young lad called the ambulance on his mobile.
5 Another driver said he saw a car driving away very fast.
6 No one caught the number of the car.

UNIT 18
Get ready
1 The cat ate five pizzas and then was sick.
2 The cat ate five pizzas and so it was sick.
3 The cat was sick as a result of eating five pizzas.
4 Because the cat ate five pizzas, it was sick.
5 After the cat ate five pizzas, it was sick.

Let's practise

6 My grandmother gave me some money, because it was my birthday.

7 I wrote my grandmother a thank-you letter, or rather I sent her a text.

8 I'm saving up for new boots, which I'll buy at the same superstore.

9 It'll be next year before I have enough money.

10 Do you know how much those boots cost, in the sale?

11 I don't expect that I can afford them, especially the black ones.

Have a go

12 because it was my birthday

13 or rather I sent her a text

14 which I'll buy at the same superstore

15 before I have enough money

16 how much those boots cost

17 that I can afford them

How have I done?

Spelling

1 batches, follies, donkeys, stereos, dresses, halves

2 invent or prevent, intend or contend, partake or mistake or uptake, impossible, insoluble, unhelpful

3 helping, playing, batting, hoping, hopping, shopping

4 played, hopped, hoped, batted, wilted, failed

5 carried, angrily, hurrying, busily

6 receive, deceive, seize, siege, shield, piece

7 abolition, extension, intention, addition, multiplication, division

8 musician, magician, beautician

9 It's, it's, its, it's, it's

10 who's, whose, whose

Grammar

11 He asked where all this was leading them. She answered that it was helping them to write better.

12 Grass is eaten by the cows. The cows are milked by the farmers. The milk is sent (by the farmers) to the dairy. The milk is put in cartons (by the dairy). The milk is bought from shops.

13 The farmers feed the cows with grass, milk them, and then send the milk to the dairy. The dairy puts the milk in cartons, which we then buy in shops.

14 The cows eat grass. The farmers milk the cows. They send it to the dairy. The dairy puts it in cartons. We buy it from shops.

15 Solid: adjective, noun. Through: preposition. Past: preposition, noun. Bat: noun, verb.